How to Be Average

An Average Book for Average Creatives

Devyn Fraser Price

For permission requests, write to the author at: devynlprice@gmail.com

How to Be Average / Devyn Fraser Price—1st ed.

Paperback ISBN 978-1-956989-19-9
Hardcover ISBN 978-1-956989-18-2

Contents

Introduction

I am a productivity nerd. Before 2020, and even through parts of it, I had my systems and goals down perfectly. I have ADHD, so the systems I put into place acted as a sort of scaffolding for the chaos that was going on in my brain.

Over the years, I have perfected a series of scaffoldings amalgamating several productivity systems that I had learned, relearned, implemented, organized, and integrated into my life.

I wrote my SMART goals, worked my way backward with deadlines, and got out a calendar with multi-colored highlighters. I set out a series of tasks to do each day to lead me up to the big fat goal. I scheduled marathons, college degrees, music performances, novel writings, and kids' school activities. My calendar looked more lit up than a Griswold's Christmas home.

I spent my time full of anxiety, running from one goal to another. Whenever something would happen that would put a spanner in my perfect plans, I would go into full panic mode—or I would completely ignore the problem until it became a bigger problem. If I got sick during marathon training, I would stress—most likely prolonging my sickness and making me miss my training for longer. I felt like I was spinning plates, knowing that if someone gave me one more plate in my perfectly choreographed performance, they'd all come crashing down.

Then 2020 happened. COVID became a pandemic. The world shut down.

I had more plans. To run the Houston marathon for the first time, form my own band, and get some gigs. To record my own album and get it out there. To finish editing and publish my novel. To revive my acting career and get out and start auditioning again. When COVID hit, so much of that became impossible. My running group canceled the marathons when we stopped gathering. Gigs were no longer available; theaters were closed. My children were home in our open plan house, which meant no quiet for recording, no chance for concentration in learning my piano pieces, and very little for writing.

I realized that there were goals that I had made that were not in my control. I had to come face to face with the fact that I could not control everything. Still, I was determined. I knew things were in my control, so I kept working out and running at home and learning more about songwriting. Because of COVID, classes for Broadway performers that were usually only available in New York City were now available to me in Houston, Texas. I continued to make goals for myself, piling on more and more work. If I couldn't control the venue in which that shared my outcome, I could control my development as an artist and athlete, right?

Then my back went out at the end of 2020. Three herniated discs, a genetic issue, I learned later. I could not walk more than a few minutes at a time, let alone run or work out. Even doing simple singing performances for my Broadway classes was difficult. On top of that, helping my children get through this time with virtual schooling was like taking on another job, and my time to develop as an artist became even less. Suddenly, things that seemed in my control weren't at all. I couldn't even control what my body did.

So as I was laid out on my sofa on Christmas in pain, I realized that my body had done what it needed. I was not listening to it. It tried to whisper to me months before, but I had ignored it. It needed me to slow down. Take it easy and listen. Be receptive. Take care of myself and my family. Stop always trying to prove myself: move forward, make goals, and just enjoy life.

As I sat and wrote in my journal, I wondered what I had achieved in life so far. If I didn't have any goals, I wouldn't get anywhere. Hell, at 38 years old, I had done nothing with my life, barely able to walk and nothing to show for my efforts: no band gigs, no album, no book, no thriving business.

I decided to list the things I had done in my life. At first, that list started with some items I thought were things you were supposed to achieve to be cool, interesting, and successful. I traveled to and lived in Europe; I ran marathons, ultra marathons, and half marathons. I got a few college degrees. I got married. I gave birth to two wonderful children.

From there, I started writing down things I felt proud of. I adopted two rescue dogs. I faced my extreme fear of heights on a 50-foot ropes course. I planted a garden that produced food my family could eat and enjoy.

And then, I listed the smaller things in life I enjoyed and appreciated, things I would miss if I had only had a day left to live. I have smelled roses, I have blown the seeds of a dandelion, I have watched a dog having the time of its life rolling in the mud, I have watched fields of heather blowing in the wind, I have seen gorgeous sunsets, I have walked on the beach, I have eaten lunch by a waterfall.

I realized that I had achieved so much. I have lived. Just because I don't have the fame and fortune society expects from me to be a successful and productive person doesn't mean I am not a successful and productive person. I have lived, and I will continue to live.

I decided at that point to write this book. To share with other creatives that it is okay to be okay with where you are, that you don't have to keep going in that straight line trajectory up and up and up with no stopping, no resting, no playing, no enjoying. You have to wear every hat—artistic genius, marketer, editor, accountant, lawyer. That it's okay to still be in a place where you're finding your voice; you can live your life the way it is now; enjoy your life the way it is now. Life is cyclical. There are times to rest and times to work. We need to know our bodies and the seasons, work with those and maintain what we have, nurture what we have right now and ultimately work toward a greater good, not to make money for some entitled guy at the top but to better the planet and everyone on it. And it starts with where you are now.

How to Read This Book

You can use this book any way you decide. The intention of this book is not to be another obligation, something you feel bad for not doing. If you wish to read it front to back in one sitting or even use it as a coaster for your coffee table, you are using it correctly.

I wrote this book as a book of inspiration. I hope you will read it in sections, pondering what you read, using the journal prompts and activities, and then carrying these principles to your creative endeavors.

Important Note

This is a book of inspiration. It is not a substitute for treatment by a qualified medical professional.

Part One: Start Where You Are

Chapter One:
It's Okay to be Average

It's an insult to be average. Go ahead, tell the next person you see that they're average, and see how they react. Take a moment and notice your own reaction to telling yourself that you're average. You probably felt some resistance, a sort of wall going up, an immediate reactive defensiveness that felt like, "I know you are, but what am I?"

Chances are, however, that you are average. Pretty much most people are. That's what average is. If everyone were outliers, the outliers would be average, so you see, mathematically, there has to be a large number of average people. And that's okay. That's a good thing. It's completely natural.

There are so many benefits to being okay with being average. Being okay with being average means you feel okay with who you are. You don't have a constant nagging feeling of being inadequate. You can let go of the stress of perfection. You'll save time, money, and energy by not giving in to the need to be in the in-crowd, to follow trends, or indulge in vices. You will feel free to create on your terms because you wouldn't feel the need to impress or compete with others.

Dr. Tomas Chamorro-Premuzic writes in *Psychology Today*, "If you want to avoid most physical and psychological illnesses, being average is one of your best options; pathology is generally associated with statistical infrequency." [1] Striving to be more than average, to the point where you frequently become anxious and worried negatively affects your health. And as we learned in the previous chapter, that constant anxiety affects your creativity.

In fact, desiring to be extraordinary will only lead to unhappiness. As philosopher and writer Alan Watts said in his 1951 book *The Wisdom of Insecurity: A Message for an Age of Anxiety*:

> The brain is in pursuit of happiness, and because the brain is much more concerned about the future than the present, it conceives happiness as the guarantee of an indefinitely long future of pleasures. Yet the brain also knows that it does not have an indefinitely long future, so that, to be happy, it must try to crowd all of the pleasures of paradise and eternity into the span of a few years." [2]

Painter Mark Rothko, Poet Sylvia Plath, Musician Janis Joplin, Actor Freddie Prinz, and Writer Ernest Hemingway are just a few examples of other creatives who left this world with great art but ultimately were unhappy. Do you think their art was worth it to them? Just because artists make great art, it doesn't mean that their lives were fulfilling and great. What are you searching for when you want to be better than average? Is your art, or rather recognition for your art, worth giving up a happy and fulfilled life? Even if you manage to become more than the average, as long as you want to be more than what you are now, you will always bring with you that feeling of not being enough.

You are probably still feeling that defensiveness at being average. Part of that is cultural upbringing. From early on, the best and brightest receive awards. Academic and physical strength receive rewards. Being the best, fastest, and strongest are virtues. We learn to stand out and be the best, so it's natural not to want to be average.

Don't worry. Even if you are average, you're still unique. There is no one in the world like you, no one with your unique set of genetics, upbringing, and environment. So even if you're average, no one can bring the unique perspective you can into this world. But if you keep trying to fill that hole, if you can't be happy until you are the best and the greatest at something, then you will spend the rest of your life trying to reach a finish line that doesn't exist. You will create art for the sake of getting noticed rather than for yourself.

Artist Spotlight

Google Shad's Black Averageness and listen to how he spotlights the benefits (and struggles) of a creative who is okay with being okay and how it intersects with race in America.

Chapter Two:
Getting Noticed

As for writing this book, a quick Google search for "getting noticed" gives me about 348 million results, and a search for "standing out" gives me 1.9 billion results. Does anyone else notice the irony here? There are books, blogs, podcasts, and social media posts everywhere, all trying to stand out and get noticed by us so they can tell us how to stand out and get noticed.

Going on Twitter is like walking down the street on a summer's day and hearing the birds all calling to each other, talking over one another, trying to attract a mate, but no one really listening. I wonder if that's why it's called Twitter. Just a bunch of noise, everyone trying to be heard but not really listening.

Facebook, Instagram, and other social media platforms rely on us to compare ourselves constantly to others, to obsessively check if someone "likes" our comments, our pictures, or our creations. Because if they don't, if we don't get noticed, then what? Are we unworthy?

The need to be noticed ties in with an age-old capitalistic idea of individualism. Individualism leads to self-expression, which leads to striving to express that individualism through commodities. "Our possessions are a major contributor to and reflection of our identities," argues Russell W. Belk, current professor of Marketing at Schulich School of Business. "Possessions are an important component of a sense of self." [1] While Belk likely wrote his study to support this relationship between consumer and brand, there is a darker side to this trend.

These days, clothes, music, brands, and even social media likes allow us to express our individualism. Companies that benefit from our need to express ourselves continue to feed into this fear that we will be average if we don't buy their products or post on their platforms. This late capitalist-led idea of individualism has become so heavily rooted in our culture that we feel bad when we don't have the latest and best products or we don't have the time or energy to post on social media platforms.

We have forgotten that the true expression of ourselves lies in our own minds and not the outward image we display to others. Our feelings and thoughts result from an infinite number of causes and effects that have led to this moment, and our creative works are the output of those thoughts and feelings. Not how many likes we get or what we spend our money on.

Have you ever stopped to wonder *why* we need to stand out and get noticed? We fall over ourselves, trying hard to be the next big thing, feeling like we're less than worthy if no one pays attention. And for what? Truly stop and think about this. We live in a competitive society, where we learn having the edge over someone else will get us ahead in life. If we stand out, we will get the girl; we will get the money; we will get into that college, on that team, get that job. Those things are likely true. You will have to stand out from the crowd to get a role in the latest Broadway show. To get paid for your novel, someone will have to notice it and want to pay you for it.

But have you ever truly questioned if you need those things? Yes, you need money to survive. That is unfortunate, given in our current economic climate. And to have money, you will need to have someone notice you enough to pay you what they think your work is worth to them. In that case, consistent creative output (or a day job) is necessary. But let's say you have the basics of what you need. You have a roof over your head. You have the money to pay the bills, at least enough to pay the basics for you to live and eat. What's missing?

I'm trying to say that we feel like something is missing, and if we can get noticed, we will be part of that crowd. We will be the best, we will have money, and people will love us so that we will fulfill that yearning desire to have lived a worthy life.

You may have, at this point, heard of FOMO or "Fear of Missing Out." A study published by scientists at Carleton and McGill University found that first-year university students suffered negative effects from FOMO, including "fatigue, stress, physical symptoms, and decreased sleep."* Stress and fatigue raise cortisol levels which can, according to an article published in Health and Human Services out of Touro University, "disrupt synapse regulation, … can kill brain cells and even reduce the size of the brain." [2] The prefrontal cortex, the area of the brain responsible for cognitive thinking and creativity, is negatively affected merely by worrying about missing out.

Imagine that you have "made it." Imagine that you have gotten noticed, and now you are an in-demand creative. You get calls for more and more of your work. You get likes and comments. You are one of the A-Listers in your field. Imagine now the work you will need to do to maintain that image. Imagine the demands on your time and the sacrifices you will need to make to meet those demands. Imagine the travel, the phone calls, the negative reviews and comments, and the media misquoting and misrepresenting your intentions. Imagine the pressure to create and create well just to maintain your status. Now ask yourself, will you be happy? Will all of your desires be fulfilled? Or do you imagine that you will be stressed, unfocused, and full of anxiety trying to reach those demands?

I'm not saying that you shouldn't go for it or that this level of recognition is necessarily bad, and you should avoid it at all costs. What I'm getting at is that if you are not satisfied with your life right now as it is, can you honestly say that you will be satisfied with your life when you have more on your plate? Really think about it. Will the parts of your life that you are unsatisfied with follow you even when you reach your Ultimate Goal?

The more we desire, the more pain we feel. Wanting more will not cure you of desire. You will simply keep desiring more even when you reach that goal, even if you are at the top level of your field. Your desires, anxieties, and fears will follow you wherever you go.

Simply by fearing being unnoticed, not part of the in-crowd, we suffer physically and mentally. We cannot live a fulfilling life if we are busy worrying about being "just average."

Journal Prompt

Take that thought experiment earlier where you were an A-lister in your field and all of the obligations and stressors that come with that job. Now imagine the opposite. Imagine that you have no obligations whatsoever. Imagine that the world keeps turning, but you can just enjoy being. What will you do with your time? Do you have energy? How do you feel in your body? What can you create? What would it feel like to enjoy missing out rather than fearing it?

Chapter Three:
Hero Worship

I sometimes lose myself in my heroes. I grab hold of some artist or celebrity who goes recognized for doing the things I really want to do, and I don't let go. I obsess over their works and their lives. I scour interviews and biographies, looking for the clue that tells me what they are doing that I'm not; what created that spark and kept it burning; how it is that they are famous and I am not.

Now I've heard that comparing myself to others is a trap, and yet, it's one I fall into again and again. If they are out there doing what they love and getting recognized for it, then there must be something they're doing right and I am doing wrong.

Maybe this is true. Perhaps they are more talented than I am. Maybe they are more confident. Maybe they knew the right people. Maybe that had more resources or better education. Maybe they had more time. Any of that could be true. But the more I learn about my creative heroes, the more

I realize that there is rarely a common thread. There's no secret morning routine or creative checklist that every single one of them follows.

I once heard a podcast featuring Rivers Cuomo, lead singer and songwriter for Weezer. He had a very detailed routine for creating songs that included cross-referencing spreadsheets. He laid out exactly how he wrote songs in such intense detail that you'd think he cracked the songwriting code. I tried to follow the same steps that he did and found that everything I wrote fell flat. I couldn't write anything good, and what's worse, I didn't have fun doing it. And certainly, as of writing this book, none of my music has ever won a Grammy.

The point is that what works for one person often doesn't work for another. And if there isn't some formula for success, then perhaps success (at least how we tend to define it as a society) is completely random.

Stories of heroes that defeat the odds are so deeply rooted in our culture that we often don't even realize how much of it we bring into our own daily lives. Today, we are obsessed with celebrities, superheroes, politicians, and other larger-than-life figures. We follow them on social media, wearing their likeness on our clothes, wondering what crazy antics they're up to and what kinds of things they eat for breakfast.

Why are we obsessed with them? Because more than anything else, we want to be like them. We have some crazy notion that these people, fictional or not, have some meaning in their lives that we don't have. Some spark that we never got, but maybe, just maybe, we could have if we tried hard enough, if we emulated them, maybe if we had the same exact kind of oatmeal they had, maybe if the same radioactive spider bit us -

So we keep these heroes in our pockets, on our screens, on our minds constantly as we strive to have what they have, be who they are, never feeling like we add up because we aren't where they are, we don't have what they have. We always want more, more, more, trying to get just a bit of what they have because then, and only then, will we be happy.

We also forget that heroes have to make sacrifices, often sacrifices that we aren't willing to make ourselves. We want to have the looks, career, health, home, family, talent, fame, and money—all of that with absolutely no sacrifices on our part. Think of the heroes you love right now, fictional or not. How many of them are truly happy with where they are now? Odds are,

there aren't a whole lot, no matter how rich or famous or decked out with superpowers. There's always something more over the next rainbow. Once they have that, then they will truly be happy.

I have had voice students who have come to me upset that they don't sound just like their heroes. One student, in particular, wanted to be just like his ultimate Rock Star hero and was upset that his voice didn't sound like his hero's. I pointed out to him that his favorite musician was not happy with his life or who he was and that he tried to be something he wasn't. Why sacrifice your love of who you are and where you are in life to emulate someone who was so unhappy? When I put it that way, my student realized that he actually wanted to be happy and redirected his energies into finding his own style with his own voice. Of course, there's nothing wrong with studying your heroes, with finding techniques that they used that you'd like to use in your own work, but don't confuse those techniques with the answers that unlock the code that will catapult you to hero status.

Moreover, we often only see the "highlight" reel for our heroes. In super-hero movies, we see the fast track to success—the totally average science nerd who gets bitten by a spider and is suddenly a crime-fighting hero—the average scientist who gets struck by lightning and can now run to Cairo in a few seconds. We see the montage for Rocky that takes all of the lengths of a motivating song for him to be ready to win the fight. Most biographies I've read of my real-life heroes skip over the part with the hard work and struggles and go straight to the Big Break. You never get to see how it is that they got that one gig that changed their life. It's one page of struggles, and *poof* their band plays on the radio.

We also tend to dismiss privilege. One common thread I found with many of my heroes is that they are male, childless, and went to college. Many of these men met other men in college and had all the free time and financial support in the world to collaborate on projects that eventually got them to a place of recognition and creative space. Many creatives in the past often had a wife or some other (invisible) support that allowed them the time and energy they needed to focus on their work.

29

How are we supposed to compete with that? Well, we don't. We can't because life doesn't work that way. We have to make sacrifices to get what we want, and if we aren't willing to make those sacrifices, then we have to recognize that our priorities may not match those of our heroes.

And that's okay.

We have to be careful with our heroes. We have to recognize the random patterns that led to their so-called success and the differences in their privileges and priorities. We need to realize that it's okay if our lives look different.

With all of this hero worship, even further entrenched in our culture with the advent of social media and back-to-back cinema superhero epics, it's hard to be okay with being average. Getting bombarded with these celebrities and heroes so much more often than any past generation makes it difficult to accept who we are in the moment.

Creative Activity

Rather than focusing on your favorite creatives as people and trying to emulate their routines and success, try focusing on their work alone. Focus on your own work using different techniques from different artists you admire. Try out what I call The Frankenstein List.

List out all of your favorite creatives and look into their works. What is it about their work that you admire? What techniques do they use that drew you to them in the first place? Write out what each specific creative does that you like.

For example, for my fiction, I like Ernest Hemingway's ability to use as few words as possible to convey an emotion. I like Toni Morrison's ability to use ordinary objects to create a sense of the extraordinary. I like Gabriel Garcia Marquez's use of color and other senses to create a painting with words. By studying these techniques and bringing them to my own work, I let go of the fact that all of these authors have won Nobel Prizes in literature. I'm focused on my work and how I can combine all these techniques to create my own creative monster.

Chapter Four:
Accepting the Whole

How often have you been told to let go of your negativity and be positive? I'm an avid lover of yoga, but I can't tell you how many times I've sat in a yoga class and heard the teacher ask me to let go of all those negative thoughts, leave them at the door, and breathe in only positivity.

Sure, it's a nice thought, and there's nothing wrong with letting a more positive perspective into your life. But we've gotten a little obsessed with this whole positivity thing of late. The problem with ignoring the negative and seeing only the positive is that life doesn't work that way.

In 1959, Victor Frankl's *Man's Search for Meaning* quoted one of Frankl's colleagues, Edith Weisskopf-Joelson, the then professor of psychology at the University of Georgia, "our current mental-hygiene philosophy stresses the idea that people ought to be happy, that unhappiness is a symptom of maladjustment. Such a value system might be responsible for the burden of unavoidable unhappiness increased by unhappiness about being unhappy."[1] In other words, we treat happiness as the default. And if happiness is the default, that must mean that any unhappiness or negativity in our life must be a problem to be solved. Striving to solve a problem that doesn't exist, or at least is not the problem we perceive it to be, will lead to unhappiness in and of itself.

There isn't only one side to everything. Life isn't only youth, spring, sunshine, health, and happiness. It's also death, winter, rain, illness, and sorrow. And that's okay. It's all part of the same whole, something to be celebrated.

Your wealth lies in both halves. To get a beautiful garden, you must first have dirt, rot, and waste. Below the gorgeous blooming flowers lies the death of a thousand other flowers that have decayed to allow the flower to bloom in the first place.

To fill that hole in yourself, you need to accept yourself for who you are right here right now, as scary as it may be. That includes the messy, the neurotic, the angry, the weak, the imperfect, the broken, and every aspect of yourself and your life that you see as negative.

The more you push that "negativity" aside and try to ignore it, the more it will whisper to you in the darkness, gnawing at you from the periphery. Denying the existence of this part of you will not make it go away.

If you stop struggling against the darker parts—your fears, your negativity, your traumas - you can relax and get curious about these aspects. This can give us some breathing room. You can relax and create some space. When you acknowledge these aspects of yourself, you cast a light on these shadows, and you realize that maybe they aren't so scary after all, like the scary shadows on your wall as a child that turn out just to be the branches of the tree in the daylight. If you can see that these things aren't so scary, you can start to accept them for what they are and even welcome them as an aspect of yourself, as welcome as those aspects you usually deem as positive. Not trying to fix anything, not trying to turn the "negative" into a "positive," merely noticing and accepting as a whole. After all, death brings life, winter brings spring, rain brings growth, illness makes room for health, and sorrow shows us how precious happiness is. All are equally needed.

I once watched a TedX video of one of my favorite creatives, Taika Waititi [2]. He gave a talk on creativity and what really caught my attention was when he mentioned that he, a half-Jewish kid growing up in New Zealand, used to draw Swastikas as a child. He didn't know why; he would just draw them everywhere, all over the place. It brought him such shame, and he would hide his drawings by turning them into windows on houses. It became an obsession the more he became ashamed of it. If you know Taika Waititi's work, you know that he eventually explored that darker obsession when he made the acclaimed film Jojo Rabbit. The film follows a young boy named Jojo, a member of the Hitler Youth who decides to become the best member of the Hitler Youth he can be. Jojo, along with his imaginary friend version of Hitler, eventually finds a Jewish girl hidden by his mother in their attic. Throughout the film, we can see that by further exploring the dark parts of this child's imagination, he comes to realize that what he thought was the evil monster turns out to be a saving grace. And Waititi's exploration of his own past obsession turned out to be a great work of art. As Pema Chodron says in one of my all-time favorite books, Start Where You Are, "When we don't act out, and we don't repress, then our passion, our aggression, and our ignorance become our wealth." [3] When we stop worrying about how ashamed, how hurt, how angry, how negative we are, and we see it as part of who we are, we begin to see the beauty of who we are as a whole.

By allowing yourself to open up and get curious about your struggles and darker parts, you start tearing down the defenses you build around it. We become softer and more vulnerable, but we become stronger because of it.

"Vulnerability is the birthplace of innovation, creativity, and change," Brene Brown says in her TedXHouston talk in 2010. [4] By digging into this part of yourself, you find the messy parts that we all share in the end. We all struggle. We all have trauma. We all wrestle with the darkness inside of us. And by letting it out, you help others to examine and ultimately accept themselves for who they are and what they can, too, offer the world. You set off a chain reaction of events that help to create a better and more caring world. That, my friend, is productivity worthy of a cause.

When you find yourself feeling out of sorts, maybe your depression or your anxiety is getting the best of you. Recognize the feeling as part of you, as part of the whole, and tell yourself, "it's okay to feel this way." Know that you are not alone and that by being vulnerable, you are helping others to navigate their own darker corners.

Activity

Next time you are feeling scared, angry, negative, or ashamed, close your eyes and notice what you're feeling in your body. What happens if you shine a light on those thoughts instead of pushing them away? Watch your thoughts and feeling and see where they go.

Chapter Five: Your Did List

Everyone's talking about the to-do list, shopping lists, and checklists. There's an entire book about lists by Atul Gawande called *The Checklist Manifesto: How to Get Things Right*. Don't get me wrong. I'm a big fan of lists. I think it's a great idea to get all the swirling thoughts out of your head and down onto paper so you don't forget them, especially if other people are depending on you to remember things. Check out Gawande's book when you get a chance.

But most lists that we tend to focus on are lists of things we need to do, endless pieces of paper or screens filled with task after task, item after item of more and more stuff to fill our lives with. We rarely focus on the things we have already done or achieved.

That's why I prefer a Did List.

There are two kinds of Did Lists that I like to keep around. One is a short-term did list. At the end of the week, I tend to fill a list with things I have achieved over the course of that week while my memory is still fresh. I use Trello to keep track of the things I need to do so that I don't forget things like making doctor's appointments or learning songs to perform. I have a Did List next to my other lists that I move my items to when I have done them. I review them at the end of each week, so I have a visual of everything I managed to do. Before I did this, I used to think I was lazy and didn't get much done. The Did List proved to me that I actually do a lot. I think we tend to have a bias toward all the things we haven't done and can easily dismiss the things we have. I recommend getting your own short-term Did List so that you can see that, actually, you're not quite as lazy as you might think.

The other Did List is more long-term and reads a bit more like a journal entry. This list involves a nice quiet place to sit and relax with a warm drink and listing all of the things you have achieved in your life that make you feel good about yourself for having done.

Here's the caveat, though. The things that you put on your Did List aren't things that you feel you should be proud of for doing. Sent such and such email, went down to the post office, and paid that bill. Those should go on your short-term weekly list. If you do feel proud of doing those things, by all means, put that on your long-term list. What I'm talking about putting on your list here are the things that truly made you feel like you lived. Things like smelling ten different kinds of flowers in the bouquet at the store, tasting freshly ripened strawberries at the farmer's market, sitting out in the sun and soaking up vitamin D, petting a dog and making him smile at you, making silly faces at a child you didn't know across the room. Things that, if you were lying on your deathbed right now, would make you lay back in satisfaction of a life well-lived. Or things that if you had one day left to live, you would go and do right this second.

At first, filling this list may seem hard, but you may find it has a sort of snowball effect, and your experiences start coming faster and faster, opening up memories of other experiences. They don't even have to be feel-good items. Living through a pandemic, or a hurricane, or one of the biggest man-induced disasters during a winter storm in Texas… not great experiences at the time, but the kinds of things you tell as stories to your great-grandchildren down the line.

You may find, after a while, that you have done more than you thought you had, achieved more than you thought because you stopped thinking of achieving by someone else's standards and started thinking of living by your own.

Part Two: Slowing Down

Chapter Six: Unsustainable

I live in America, where productivity is considered one of the highest virtues. Productivity is rooted in the American Puritan tradition. That tradition sees idle hands as sinful. Busy hands were closer to God. During the Industrial Revolution, usefulness and productivity took a stronger hold in the Western world. Even children's books and television programs in the twentieth century regurgitated the need to be useful. Any parent of a young child who loves trains will tell you how Thomas the Tank Engine and his friends only yearned for one thing in life—to be useful. To be useful meant to be worthy.

Now that we have the internet and social media, now that we are connected to each other all over the world at all times, now that we remain plugged in 24/7, we are expected to be producing at all times. Vast empires build themselves on productivity for the sake of productivity. Systems, apps, coaches, and books on productivity are ubiquitous, ready to help you be a worthy and useful human being. It has become less about producing something for the good of humanity, such as food and resources that we need to live and thrive, and more about being busy for the sake of being busy.

Why do we continue to feel like we need to fill every moment in life with some sort of development? Why do we need to check our email at all hours, have notifications for our texts, to have a "side hustle" in addition to our normal jobs? Why do we feel guilty if we're not filling up our free time with "doing something productive?" What are we hoping to achieve? What is the ultimate goal?

The prevailing theme in economics all over the world is growth. Governments in most countries measure their success on how much growth there is. Currently, growth is defined by how many goods and services the population produces as well as the increased value of those goods and services. I'm not an economist, but I often wonder if the end game of these growth-based economics is just to increase the value of the goods and services or if it's taken into account that these goods and services need to, in return, help the population thrive. If so, what would the definition of a thriving population be outside of increasing productivity?

If most nations base their success on growing Gross Domestic Product (GDP), then the only thing we can do to be successful citizens of that nation would be to help increase that GDP. But what do we get in return? The idea of the growth of production may be to improve our standard of living, but what is our standard of living based on? Is it our ability to consume? If we are constantly producing and consuming at an increasing rate, how long can we, as a species, last? How long can the planet take our continued consumption of resources to maintain that growing cycle of production and consumption? To quote Muse, one of my all-time favorite bands, "An economy based on endless growth is unsustainable."

Interestingly enough, there are attempts to rectify this situation. The nation of Bhutan has created an alternative to GDP called GNH, or Gross National Happiness. The idea is that the nation's ultimate goal is to increase the population's happiness and overall well-being. There are a number of businesses right now that are focusing on sustainability. Many investors require businesses to have a strategy to promote sustainability and a plan to decrease environmental impact. My husband currently works in agricultural data and has found that research on and education on sustainable farming has increased. What sustainability means as an end goal remains vague, but it's becoming apparent to many that we are driving toward a future on an increasingly empty tank of gas.

All of this trickles down into your own life. Unfortunately, you can't simply take a step outside of this current growth-driven society, but you can help decrease your individual workload. Chances are, besides trying to put food on the table to survive, there's not much more beyond that. But if you're alive, you are already doing a pretty good job.

But the feeling of needing to be busy is strong and isn't easily shaken. We may never in our lifetimes feel a hundred percent okay with just being. But you can help ease that burden by slowing down a little, by lightening the load of work you feel you need to do. By doing so, you may introduce a sense of sustainability in your life and in your work.

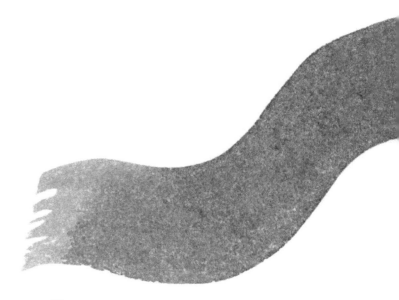

So how can you slow down? What can you do to help get some breathing room into your schedule? Here are a few tips to follow:

1. Say no to everything you possibly can. Even if it looks tempting and shiny, say no.

2. Drop anything that you can live without. If it is not a priority, you don't need to do it. Even if you paid for it, consider it a sunk cost (or consider it paying for some sanity).

3. Make a list of all the things left to do that have an ending. The things that if you got done right now, you'd have finished them forever. Do those the first chance you get. Don't put them on the back burner unless they're not important. If they're un-important, you don't need to do them.

4. Make a list of all the things left to do that have an end date. Put them in your calendar and either

forget about them until that time or put them on a repeating to-do list and do a little each day until that date.

5. Everything else that is ongoing, prioritize. Do the things that can be done quickly as soon as you possibly can, and then you don't have to think about them for the rest of the day. The things that need doing at a certain time, put them on your calendar or to-do list, and then forget them until it's time to deal.

6. Do not say yes to anything else—do not make any more commitments until you get your existing commitments down to a reasonable amount. If it's still too much, rinse and repeat.

7. Ask for help. We are social creatures. It is in our DNA. There is no shame in asking for help, nor is it a sign of weakness. It is natural. Asking for help is an act of humanity.

Chapter Seven:
Playing the Social Game

Times seemed so much easier before social media. Growing up in the 90s, I had a small circle of immediate friends I would see at school or the mall. They'd come to my house, or I'd go to theirs. Then I'd go home and spend my evenings listening to music or reading. I could do stupid stuff, and no one but that close circle needed to know. I could write poems or song lyrics that I never felt the need to share with anyone. I wrote them because I wanted to. Sure, I dreamt of being some big-shot actor/writer/rock star, but it was a far-off dream. I never felt I had to write, act, or sing well immediately. I never felt like I had to constantly stay in contact with my friends and share my work with them to stay relevant.

These days, creators have to not only create their work but also regularly create it on a schedule. They have also to create content around their field. They have to be an editor, publisher, curator, designer, accountant, lawyer, promoter… the list goes on. The way most social media platforms set up algorithms, an artist would have to create a vast amount of content daily just to get their work seen.

Don't get me wrong. Social media can be a great tool. I've met some really fantastic friends online that I'm still good friends with decades later because we keep in touch on social media. I've come across some great writers and artists I likely wouldn't have otherwise.

But we all know by now that social media can be a curse. Not only can social media be terrible for our minds as consumers, but it can really affect us negatively as creators.

A study published in Scientific Reports found that social media addiction can alter brain structure, reducing grey matter in the amygdala (the area of the brain associated with emotions), similar to gambling addicts.[1] This alteration can lead to an increase in impulsive behavior, emotional disorders, and anxiety. Because of this physical and (and by proxy) chemical alteration in the brain, feelings of anxiety and impulsiveness are present even when trying to do something else.

I can't tell you the number of times I've turned off my phone, turned on webpage blockers, and sat down to do something creative, only to find that I couldn't focus. And because I couldn't focus, I would become anxious and feel like a failure. And because I felt like an anxious failure, I would turn back to social media to soothe these feelings.

Anxiety and lack of focus caused by social media addiction lead to more social media consumption. It becomes a vicious cycle. Dr. Phil Reed, Professor of Psychology at Swansea University, wrote in Psychology Today, "while many people who use social media a great deal are anxious when they are not using social media, they turn to social media to reduce this 'withdrawal' anxiety and end up with another form of anxiety produced by engaging with their digital platforms." [2]

This can lead the creator to be burnt out, unable to create because of the need to keep up with new technology, platform changes, and just the daily grind. So many artists are exhausted and just want to create.

What drives the need to stay relevant via social media? As discussed previously, the need to stand out, be noticed, and be the best—to keep from being average.

You can opt out of all of this. You do not have to follow the same route as everyone else. If this social media grind leaves you feeling drained, is it worth it to keep going that route? I know for me, it's not. I know I will only start to feel exhausted, bitter, and empty.

You can do a few things to avoid the whole social media game when it comes to your work. Of course, you can always stop sharing your work. If you don't depend on money for your work, why go through all that hassle? Start creating just for yourself. If you feel like sharing, share it, but only do it on your terms. Creating work on your terms is a rebellious act. Turn your own work into an act of rebellion.

If this doesn't resonate with you, or if you're looking for a way to make some extra money, you can try these few tips for marketing without social media (or, in some cases, even a web presence).

Go to a conference in your field and share your work there. Some conferences have booths in which you can display and sell your work.

1. Do some busking. Busking isn't just for musicians. You can sketch people, make them a painting on request, or write them a poem. I did a few stints of poetry busking, which was so much fun! And people walked away with a nice little poem and a smile!
2. Get your work featured at a local library, college, bookshop, or cafe. Many of those places love local artists and creators and would be happy to display works from you. I've been to some really great trendy cafes with artwork on the walls, CDs, or books by local artists for sale.
3. Share with friends and family. Keep it small. Many people in your real-life social circle may be excited to see or hear your work.
4. Teach a local class on Meetup.com or at your local library in your field and feature your work.
5. Put a link to your work in email signatures.
6. Look for local festivals and farmers' markets. You may be able to perform or feature/sell your work there.
7. Find other creatives in your field and collaborate. Maybe you can feature your work together.

These are just a few examples. Whatever resonates with you, go for it. And remember that you don't have to do any of this if you choose not to. It's okay to create for yourself and yourself alone. Bring the fun back into your creating by doing it on your own terms.

Chapter Eight: Cycles of Life

There is no such thing as linear growth. Take a look outside. Where do you see this kind of activity going on in nature? Nothing keeps going at full energy, all the time, forever. The seasons come and go, and flowers bloom and die. Animals hibernate or slow down in the winter. The sun reaches its zenith and then climbs back down again.

Humans are a part of nature, whether we want to be or not. We, too, operate in cycles. We have energy, and we're tired. We feel happy, and we feel sad. We are healthy, and we are sick. None of these states of being are wrong. They just are. Just like the plants, animals, and earth around us, we need to take moments of rest, of healing.

Are you tired and slow in the winter? Guess what? So is nearly every other animal on the planet. Don't blame yourself for feeling sluggish or down. Be grateful that you are a part of nature. Listen to your needs. Your body is telling you how things are, not how you think things should be.

Seasonal depression is real, but I feel it's made worse by the expectations society puts on us and that we put on ourselves: that we have to be going at all times, even when it's fully natural to just lay under a blanket and not do anything.

And it's not just seasonal. Sometimes, when we work too hard, we go too fast or too hard, and we need to rest. There's nothing wrong with that. We aren't machines. But even machines need to charge up after a while. We put more pressure on ourselves than on anything else, living or not.

Perhaps we can achieve a sense of sustainability by being more in tune with natural cycles. A bear hibernates during winter to reserve energy while food is scarce. That way, when spring returns and food becomes more abundant, she will have the energy to consume and produce.

To introduce sustainability into your creative life, you must reserve your energy when resources are scarce and create when you have more energy. Your creative resources are scarce if you are tired, burnt out, sick, and anxious. This is the time to go into creative hibernation.

Taking a break and resting (or maybe even hiding under a blanket for a while) would allow you to reserve your energy until more resources are available. Then, when you feel that creative spark returning, you can emerge from your hibernation slowly. Consume what gives you energy—foods that help you feel good, other creative works that inspire you, for example—then you can spend that energy creating.

When you feel your reserves deplete, repeat the process again. Join the rest of the natural world by working and living in cycles.

How can we implement this "creative hibernation?" We can start with rest, boredom, and play.

Resting

As we discussed in chapter six, productivity for the sake of productivity makes no sense. There has to be a reason we produce, and the natural reason is that we produce or create to thrive. But if you continue to produce without any sign of stopping, you reduce your health and happiness, and you stop thriving.

So what if you started to think of producing as moving in this cycle of growth and dormancy? What if there was such a thing as "rest productivity?" If you want to produce the result of thriving both in well-being and as a creative, then you need to include rest in the equation.

The point of resting is to stop, recharge, and relax.

Air, water, and food are considered the three main components to sustain life, but we don't often hear about sleep much in that equation. Going without sleep for more than a few days can be fatal. Our bodies rely on sleep to maintain life. Sleep doesn't only help us to stay focused and less stressed. When you sleep, your body removes unnecessary toxins, repairs your cells, and reorganizes your neurons, making functioning in your daily life, physically, mentally, and emotionally, much easier.

Sleep is a fantastic way to rest, but it's not the only way. If resting is to cease working, then to creatively hibernate, you need to stop working. Now I don't mean for you to go into your bedroom for three months and not come out until spring. We don't have that option, and not all animals go into deep hibernation. To rest for extended periods of time is not meant for humans. Our bodies depend on regular movement, and to maintain that regular movement, we can't shut down completely for more than hours at a time.

But there are times when we need more rest than usual. When we are sick and depleted, it makes sense to take more time to recharge.

To rest, you have to stop what you're doing. If you can stop working completely without negative consequences, then that's great. Taking some time away from working can do wonders.

Lin Manuel Miranda decided to take a vacation from the demands of working on his hit musical *In the Heights*. Instead of working, he decided to read a book while lying on the beach. The book he chose to read was a biography of Alexander Hamilton. Chances are, unless you've been asleep for the last ten years, you've heard about the hit Broadway musical that resulted in this decision to step away from work. "The moment my brain got a moment's rest," Miranda told a writer for HuffPost, "Hamilton walked into it." [1]

If you have a "day job" that is not a part of your creative work, then stop your creative work for a few days. Maybe a few weeks. Or for as long as it takes to begin feeling that need to create again. If you are not in a situation where you can completely stop working, then what can you stop? What can you take off of your plate? There are some tips in chapter six to lighten your workload so that you have more space to rest.

When you're not used to rest, this may be difficult. I have friends who have balked at the idea of rest and a few who have told me that they don't even know how to rest.

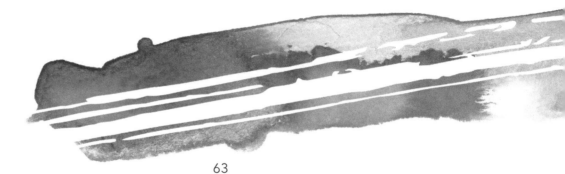

How to Rest

- Take a nap.
- Meditate.
- Walk slowly in nature.
- Take a vacation (an actual one where you don't constantly check your notifications).
- Sit in the sun.
- Declutter one space and sit in it.
- Try Yoga Nidra.
- Take a social media sabbatical.
- Watch animals in nature.
- Turn off phone notifications.
- Go on a retreat or create a retreat in your own home.
- Mindfully make and drink a cup of tea.
- Sit in a bath with the lights off.
- Lie down in the middle of the kitchen floor while your toddler pours milk on your toes. It counts.
- Take three deep breaths.

If you're not used to resting, you may feel guilty for taking time away from things you feel you must do. That's okay. Allow yourself to feel that way. Sit with that feeling and tell yourself that it's alright. And then go back to what you're doing. Each time you rest and do this exercise, it will be easier. Put this in your calendar, or do it now.

When we try to rest, we often fill that time with consumption. We watch television programs, go on social media, and eat food that makes us feel bad afterward. This kind of consumption can lead to anxiety and burnout as much as (and possibly more than) working [see my chapter on social media]. Hibernation does not include consuming. Consuming is not rest.

Get Bored

Boredom is a bad word. Our lives are centered around keeping us from being bored. We have radios (and in some cases even televisions) in our cars, phones filled with games and apps in our pockets, and video games to distract us.

Distract us from what? Boredom is uncomfortable. Boredom forces us to pay attention to feelings we don't like to experience. It's easier to distract ourselves from diving deeply into our thoughts and feelings and to replace those uncomfortable feelings of facing the void of nothingness by occupying ourselves with activities that stimulate us and give us a sense of accomplishment.

But boredom can be a good thing for creatives. I'm not talking about extended periods of boredom, which may be associated with depression and other emotional disorders. I'm talking about short periods of boredom. Taking time away from constant stimulation to delve into the deeper recesses of our thoughts and feelings.

We can't shut off our brains completely. When we force ourselves to be bored, our minds will find a way to deal with this lower level of stimulation. When we free ourselves from distraction, our brain will begin to shift gears. Daydreaming, imagination, and deep contemplation are all products of boredom. They also happen to be good fodder for creative works.

By being bored, you can shut out the overwhelming sights and sounds of modern life and begin sensing the rhythms of nature. You can begin to get to know yourself a little better, and you can use that knowledge not only to find a pattern of creating that better suits your life, but you can explore those thoughts and feelings that you had distracted yourself from in the past. Those are the dark corners that good creative works shine a light on.

How to be Bored

- Turn off music or podcasts when you drive.
- Take your phone away from your bedside so you don't pick it up at the first sign of being unable to sleep.
- Instead of watching Netflix, just sit in your living room.
- Go for a walk without headphones.
- Sit on your porch/balcony/or front step and just observe.
- Learn to meditate (meditation is a great tool for becoming comfortable with being bored).
- Eat dinner at your kitchen table without your phone or something to read.
- Take a bath and just sit.

Play

Adults are terrible at playing. But playing is serious business. Watch a child and see how engulfed in her fantasy world she is. Adults need this as well. If you have a pet or have ever watched Animal Planet, you know that it's natural for adults to play.

It's hard as humans to give ourselves permission to play. We are socialized to see playing as a waste of time. Consider how you feel when you do something you want to do, when you're not bound by musts, when you allow yourself the freedom just to do.

Chances are, any time you've played recently, even if just a little, you were in a better mood. Playing is a must. Dedicate a small amount of time to play, even if it's just for 15 minutes. Take note of how you feel afterward.

Ways to Play

I've come across a few adults who have told me they don't know how to play. They've just forgotten how to do it. That's okay. It's hard when you're out of practice. Here are a few ideas you could try out.

- Play a board game or do a puzzle.
- Play with a pet.
- Wrestle with your kids.
- Think of something you loved playing as a kid. Try doing that thing now.
- Color in a coloring book.
- Try out a local sport.
- Do a mad lib.
- Do some LARPing (Live Action Role Playing).
- Go to the craft store and pick out a project.
- Make up silly lyrics to your favorite song.

- Put together a Lego set.
- Create a bucket list and do the easiest thing on the list.
- Ask a fun friend what they like to do.
- Grab a brush, put on your favorite stadium anthem, and pretend you're fronting a rock band.
- Sit with yourself for 15 minutes, without screens, and ask yourself what you feel like doing. No matter what it is, just do it, even if it's just having a nap. How many kids have you seen falling asleep in a bowl of spaghetti*? It's natural. Just do it.

*My mother has a picture of me doing this. Feel free to ask her about it.

Part Three: Navigating the World of Productivity & Creativity

Chapter Nine:
The Case Against Goals

And while we're on goals, that is another word thrown around a lot, often hand in hand with productivity. A goal is an end to a means. Along with productivity, we are obsessed with goals to the point that it seems our goal is productivity and to be productive is to produce more goals.

Setting goals, however, is a good thing, right? Goals give us direction and focus. It gives us something to work towards. Otherwise, our existence would be aimless and meaningless. Without goals, we would be unworthy.

Say that last sentence out loud. It seems ridiculous, doesn't it? And yet, that's the underlying message when we pick apart why we create goals and why we need to be productive in the first place. Without a goal and without productivity, we are useless. And when we are useless, we are unworthy. This is a mirage. A message encoded within the messages that are blasted at us daily since childhood. Where did this notion begin? If we traced that message back, where would it lead?

I argue that we do not need productivity, and we do not need goals. At least not in the way we traditionally think we need them.

Before I get to what we can do instead, let me tell you what is wrong with goals in the first place.

Most goals are based on things we can't control. We as humans like to control things, but if we've learned anything from 2020, we've learned that there are things in life we can't control. I had a big fat goal of starting a band and getting a certain number of shows booked by the end of the year. Then COVID happened. I got a big fat 0 on that goal. Why? Because that goal based itself on things I couldn't control. I can't make people join my band. I can't force venues to stay open and book me. I can't force audiences to pay attention. And I can't help if one of my kids gets sick night after night and I have to stay home and look after them. Creating goals like getting a book traditionally published, getting a certain number of visitors to your blog, or making a certain amount of money isn't in your realm of control. Creating goals outside of your control can lead to stress, anxiety, depression, and a feeling of failure when things don't go according to your plans.

Most goals are based on comparison to others. Think about the goals you currently have. Chances are, most of them base themselves on what you think you *should* be doing. And why do you think you should be doing those things? Likely because you've seen other people doing them. Maybe your friends have achieved these things. Perhaps you've seen people you've admired achieving them. Maybe it's a cultural norm you never really questioned, like getting married, buying a house, and having 2.5 kids (also things you can't control). But if you really sat down and thought about these things, I mean really got honest with yourself, would these be things that you feel like you should be doing or things that you really do want to do? My guess is if you really were honest with yourself, most of your goals would fall into that first category.

Most goals are based on a linear timeline of a continual rate of growth. What do I mean by that? I mean that often when we make goals, we assume that everything will go the way we want it to all the time and we're going to have the same amount of energy, the same circumstances, the same money, etc. that we always will. I can't tell you how many marathon training plans I've gone through that had week after week of increased mileage with absolutely no contingency plans for injury, illness, or just plain no time. We assume we will have the same amount of energy in December as we do in June. We assume we will have the same amount of time to dedicate to something when our kids are off school as they are when they're going to band practice. And we're always shocked when something bad happens like illness, injury, or death—even though these things are a normal part of life. And failing our goals because of these things exacerbates our anxiety.

Most Goals Don't Allow Us to Innovate. Goals, especially ones with little wiggle room, don't give us time to innovate. Often when we set goals, they are set with the idea that we will not fail them. However, failure is a significant way to learn and is often frowned upon in this society. We often don't put the time to play into our goals, either. If we make a goal to finish a book on a certain deadline, chances are, we aren't going to take the time to go off on tangents, stop and stare at a wall, or go on a walk when we're stuck. Or if we did, we'd see that as a waste of time and would feel guilty. Despite that, the best ideas often come when we take time off and play.

As you can see, most goals don't allow for the nuances in life and set us up on a certain, narrowly focused track of linear thinking that leads us to a feeling of failure and unworthiness if we don't succeed. And if we do succeed, often we are left with a feeling of "well, what now?" We make another goal, repeating the process, never happy until reaching that goal. But that happiness is fleeting because we won't be happy until reaching that next goal. If you're always chasing future deadlines and experiencing each moment as a dedication to another time and place, what will you experience when you get there? Past experience likely indicates that you will again be thinking about some other moment than the one you're in.

Constantly looking into the future for your happiness can actively hurt you in the moment. When I get caught up in these visions of being a head writer or showrunner on an international hit television program or touring the world as the author of award-winning novels, I find it hard to create anything. How can anything I create now live up to the vision I have in my head of being perfect at my craft? I end up scaring myself into not creating anything in the first place. And if I can't create anything, I certainly can't end up fulfilling those future visions anyway.

But what can we do instead? Without goals, don't we just wander through life aimlessly? Well, not necessarily, but in the next chapter, I'm going to tell you why wandering through life aimlessly might not be as bad as you think.

Activity

Look over some of your current goals. Write them down on a piece of paper or in an online document. What aspects of these goals can't you control? Are any of them based on comparison to others? Do any of them take into consideration the natural cycles of life? After you've finished that, go through each one and ask yourself, what will you do once you achieve the goals? Will your life have improved? Will you be happy? Will you feel fulfilled or move on to the next goal? What use will this goal have in your life and the lives of others?

Chapter Ten:
Wanderlust for Life

I will make a confession here that is only a confession to people who don't know me. I am a huge nerd. As a teen, I loved playing Dungeons & Dragons, fantasy adventure movies, and reading fantasy novels full of elves and dragons. My favorite series growing up was called *Dragonlance*. In that series, there is a race called Kender, similar to Hobbits from *Lord of the Rings*. Both Kender and Hobbits were short with pointy ears, and they loved a good story. The main difference between Hobbits and Kender, however, was Wanderlust. Most of us have heard this term before. Wanderlust is the term we use for people who have the desire to travel the world. And the Kender did have that. But they also had something else that I think is part of Wanderlust that is rarely talked about but is an integral part of that desire to travel. That trait is curiosity.

Kender had an insatiable sense of curiosity. The kind that would get them into trouble (in the series, jail cells were often full of Kender who had wandered into places they weren't supposed to be or had pockets full of other peoples' belongings they found interesting - oops!). But that trouble didn't bother them as much as it bothered others who had very little of that childlike wonder. I think there are people in real life who have a bit of that curiosity as well. Why else would they choose to wander the world? Hopefully, not for a juicy Instagram pic.

I bring this up because I think we're all born with that innate curiosity. Babies learn to sit up, crawl, and walk not because they think, "Oh, I'd better learn to do these things, or else I'm going to fall behind." They do so because they want to reach out and grab new things they find interesting in the world. They want to see them, feel them and stuff them in their mouths to see if they taste good.

Somewhere along the way, most of us have lost that curiosity. Everything we do, even our creative pursuits, is steered by a need to be productive, to produce merely to produce, to get ahead, to be liked and noticed, not because we are curious.

When we don't get noticed, or we feel we're falling behind, we look back and wonder, "what have I done with my life? What have I achieved? Have I done nothing?"

This very moment of questioning sparked me to write this book. I was sitting at my desk, bemoaning the fact that I was going to be forty soon and had done so very little with my life. I decided to journal about how I felt about this fact, something I have been bemoaning since I was in my early twenties.

It was during that exercise that my child interrupted me. At first, I got annoyed, but then I realized I had created a human being. That was pretty cool. Actually, I created two. I began to remember all of the things I had experienced in my life. Going to live in another country with a man I met on the internet (still married sixteen years later as of writing this book). I faced my extreme fear of heights in the mountains of Georgia at Camp Nerd Fitness by doing a ropes obstacle course fifty feet in the air. I baked cakes, learned to make sourdough from scratch, saw Notre Dame (before it caught fire), grew vegetables from seed to salad, adopted rescue dogs, fronted rock bands, taught singing lessons to kids, and watched dolphins play in the Mediterranean. The list goes on.

This is not to brag or to flaunt the privilege I'm aware that I have. This is just a personal account to demonstrate that if you really sit down and think about it, you've done more than you may have realized before. Even if you've never been to another country or started a family, there are other amazing things you have done.

On my list, I included other items, things that I've gotten to experience in life that don't require vast amounts of resources. Smelling roses, eating bread fresh from the oven, wrapping up in a warm, soft blanket in the winter, seeing a shooting star. All of these things filled me with such a wonderful feeling. I realized that if I knew I would die soon, those were the things I would want to spend the rest of my life doing. At no point in my last days would I want to sit at my desk thinking about how to be productive or if anyone would like my work.

After that full list, I wrote in my journal, it seemed to me that I had done so much before 40, and I still had so much more I could do if I were lucky enough to keep going. This was the standard by which I would call myself successful.

I felt filled with newfound energy and spirit. I had only thought that my life was meaningless because I didn't produce anything outside of my normal day job that made other people notice me or that didn't make me lots of money. Those were the things I thought I was supposed to achieve to be a success.

My point is that it would seem to someone on the outside, someone who was obsessed with productivity and goals in the traditional societal sense, that I had wandered through life aimlessly. And perhaps so far, I have. But I have gotten so much out of it, and I will continue to do so, out of curiosity, out of Wanderlust for life.

That doesn't mean I don't have things I need to do. We all need to survive, but that doesn't mean we can all go around smelling roses and eating bread until we die. But maybe those things don't have to be meaningless and aimless. Maybe, they can be part of the aim, part of the journey itself.

In the meantime, I will aim to be more like the Kender I admire and let my curiosity lead my way through life.

Chapter Eleven:
Using Your Compass

With the arrival of COVID-19, the world became suddenly aware that there are a heck of a lot of things outside of our control. As a performing artist, I realized quickly that I based many of the goals I had created on things outside my control.

At first, it was immediately obvious that I couldn't control things like how many shows I could book or even when I could see my friends. But it became clear that even depending on things like industries behaving the way they had in the past was outside of my control. As I write this book, I realize that getting it published traditionally is beyond my control. Even finishing it is. For all I know, I could lose the entire book in a freak tech accident. Or I could keel over before I finish this sentence. Or society itself could crumble, leaving us to fend for ourselves, eating only local flora and fauna, the internet and the written word a distant memory in a new era of survival.

Perhaps that's an extreme notion, but it's not untrue. There are many more things outside our control than we care to admit. Not only have I realized during the COVID pandemic that I can't control events, but I also realized (a little late, I suppose) that I can't control others' thoughts and actions. And the more I try, the more helpless, anxious, and depressed I feel.

You will never get out of having obligations. And there will always be more obligations than can possibly be met. Nobody gets a free pass from this. There will always be more to do than can be done. So you can stop trying right now. You can stop trying to control your situation. You can stop trying to reach that perfect state where everything seems finished, everything is exactly where it needs to be, and no one will ever need anything from you again. That perfect state is called dead. And dead is not a very good place to be, creatively speaking.

Instead of Goals, Find a Direction.

Goals are for when everything works out perfectly. You want to run a marathon? Go for it. Just make sure you don't get injured, the race doesn't get canceled, and your life goes smoothly the whole time. If you haven't noticed yet, life doesn't work that way. No matter how much we plan, life will dump a bunch of unexpected trash all over our expectations. If we decide on a goal, plan it out, and then life kicks our legs out from under us, we're likely to feel like a failure. The story we tell ourselves is that everyone else can do it, but we aren't good enough. But this isn't the truth. By setting up expectations of events outside of our control, we are setting ourselves up for disappointment.

Instead of making elaborate plans and goals, try finding your direction. Imagine you were the captain of a ship. You plot out an exact course, but a hurricane forms in the middle of your path. If that was the only course you planned for; your only choices would be to turn back or go through the storm. However, if you knew the general direction of your destination, you could circumvent the storm or wait it out, knowing you'd eventually get to where you wanted to go. You would get out our compass and head in the right direction, no matter what storm may turn up.

So how do you know what direction to go in? Well, that is up to you and your values. What is most worthy of your time? What are your beliefs?

Once you know that, you can follow through life in that direction, pause when you need to, get knocked down if you must, then get up and start heading in that direction again.

How do you find your north? By defining your values. For some, those values might be obvious. Words may spring to mind immediately when the question "what's important to you?" is asked; that strong sense of duty and maybe pride may swell in your chest the moment you think of these, and maybe even a solitary tear springs to your eye.

For the rest of us, things may be a little murky. Maybe we thought we knew what was important, but on further investigation and meditation, we realized that we only thought they were important because those were things we felt were supposed to be important.

How do you know a good value from a not-so-good value? Good values are within your control and help make you, the people around you, and the world better. The not-so-good values you base on things outside of your control, can eventually harm others and the world, and are based on your emotional reaction rather than on solid observation.

Going in the direction of our values can be more important than the goals themselves. As I stated before, goals are often based on something we can't control, but if we follow our values, we are always in control. We can use these values to make tough decisions. If we are always following what we believe to be right, then we can't go too far off of the path.

Victor Frankl wrote, "Don't aim at success—the more you aim at it and make it a target, the more you are going to miss it." He goes on to argue that happiness will come when you dedicate yourself to a greater cause.[1]

In an interview with Conan O'Brien, I once heard Barack Obama say that when he had to make huge decisions that could impact the entire world, he would decide based on his values. He felt that as long as he was going in a direction that he felt was right, then he could say that he did his best.[2]

You could do several exercises to help you find what values are important to you and keep in mind that what may be important to you now may change. We are not static beings. We are always changing, down to the cellular level.

What we value is what we prioritize. What's important to us is how we navigate life. Believe it or not, we all have values. Right now, you are making decisions based on what's important to you. I never really thought of family as being one of my top values. It's not that I didn't value family; it just didn't spring to mind as a value at all. But I discovered that when my children truly need me for anything important, I will drop every other obligation to make sure they get my support. And I don't just value family in general. I value the well-being of my children.

If you tune into what you truly value, you can achieve a greater sense of direction in your decisions and your work. If you ever need to make a decision about which of the infinite number of obligations that vie for your attention, you can focus on the obligations that will bring you closer to your values. Your values can be your compass when you feel lost or overwhelmed.

Activity

Take some time to journal or list the things that are important to you. Not what you think should be important but what you really feel are more important than anything else. Ask yourself why you think it's important. Then ask yourself why again. Then ask why again. Ask why over and over until you can't ask why anymore. Look for patterns in how you spend your time and attention. When things in life go unexpectedly, what changes do you make first? What makes you call into work? What do you put on the back burner until things calm down?

You can look up values lists online. Brene Brown has a good one, and you can see what words stick out to you. [3] Find 15-20, and then whittle them down by combining similar words until you get 3-5. These words should be a guide, not an absolute. Use them as inspiration.

Chapter Twelve: Journey of a Thousand Actions

So you have your compass set, and now you're ready to get moving. How do you get there? It may still seem an overwhelming journey to get from one end of the globe, or one end of an intention to another, without some sort of map or goal in mind. So how do you start?

You may have heard the much-quoted proverb from the Tao Te Ching, where Lao Tsu tells us that a "journey of a thousand miles begins with a single step." Here Lao Tsu is telling us that it's easy to get caught up in the future, in the bigness of it all. A thousand miles is a lot to take in, and it's easy to get overwhelmed. But a single step. That's easy. All we have to do is put our foot forward and take it. And then we do it again. And again.

Another favorite quote of mine, along the same vein but in a more humorous way, comes from the movie Better Off Dead. When the protagonist Lane is worried about how he will ski down the infamously deadly mountain path, his helpfully simple friend Scooter offers the advice to "go that way very fast. When something gets in your way, turn."

The point is, when we set goals, we're often just overwhelming ourselves. We're looking down that deadly mountain wondering how we will get out of it all alive. But if we just start with step one and work a little at a time every day, rising to challenges as we meet them, we might be a little more equipped to handle our journey, making it a little more fun along the way.

When I ran my first marathon, it was easy to slip into the mindset of "holy crap, I'm running 26 miles. I have to run 26 miles." Every time I thought that, I got tired. Really tired. I wanted to quit. But when I thought about just putting one foot in front of the other, talking with my running buddy, and enjoying the moment, things got easier. The most enjoyable time of the marathon and the moment I had the most energy was when I passed a live band playing one of my favorite songs. I started dancing right around mile 20. I suddenly felt a surge of energy because I wasn't thinking about how many more miles I had to go or how hard running was. I was thinking about how much fun I was having.

As I took on writing this book, it was easy to fall into the overwhelmed trap. I had never written a nonfiction book before. I hadn't the slightest clue what to do. I knew there were things I had never dealt with before, things like agents and editors and queries. But if I had thought about all of those, I would not have started the project because I would have felt overwhelmed, even if I had broken it down. Even if I had broken it down in tiny steps, life would have gotten in the way—kids would have had emergencies, the house would have burned down, I would have needed back surgery - any number of things would have gotten me off course and, again, I would have been overwhelmed.

Instead, I opted for a simple action of writing. Each day, I decided to sit down and write something. This method goes along with the natural rhythms of life. If I'm feeling well, energetic, and have a lot of time on my hands, then I can sit down and write for hours, the words pouring from me. If I'm unwell, my chronic back pain flaring, the winter downers getting to me, my kids need my attention, or the words aren't coming to me, I sit, and I write a sentence or two if that's all that's coming to me. Sometimes, I think I only have a sentence or two in me, and bad ones at that, but I sit down in my chair, open up this document and find that I have a lot more to say than I thought.

I just make it a habit to sit down at my desk, open the word document and write. That's it. I do have a bit of a map in front of me. I started with writing an outline so I had some semblance of where I was going, an idea of where my compass was pointing. And when I'm done writing, I will begin editing. And when I'm done editing, I will research the next step, and when I'm done researching, I will take the next step, however big or small that may be. If all I can manage is the smallest shuffle forward, that's all I will take, and that's fine.

There's a reason the fable of the tortoise and the hare has lasted centuries. The truth is that the tortoise wins because he takes the race one step at a time. He doesn't try to keep up with the hare, even when it seems like the hare is winning. He gets there in the end because the hare, in all its need to complete the race at once, wore himself out.

I wanted to write this book because my compass points towards healing, curiosity, acceptance, and empathy. Part of heading down that path is not only helping myself through this process of being okay with where I am in life but helping to break down the structures of our current drive toward productivity for the sake of productivity and helping others who feel stuck as well. That's a lot to take on, and if I try to rush into it, I'll wear myself down before I can get anywhere. I take it one step at a time.

Activity

What is something that you could do that will take you in the direction of your values? What small steps could you take, a little at a time, that can help you down that path?

Chapter Thirteen: Paying Attention

Now, more than ever, we are bombarded by little demands for our attention in nearly every waking moment. Texts, private messages, social media, calls from work, and advertisements constantly compete for our attention.

If you tend to feel exhausted every time you read a text or scroll on social media, you are not alone. The constant demands for our attention are fracturing our thought processes and leaving us feeling depleted.

Many of us tend to feel as if we have to reach some fixed point in our lives before we can be happy. We feel we have to get to some arbitrary place in life before we can truly feel joy. Until then, life will be an unhappy struggle.

The bad news is that life will always be a struggle. Even if you do achieve those goals in life, you will only strive for something else. You'll lose weight but want to be thinner or maybe have more muscle. You'll have the money but want more. You'll get the promotion, but you have to work longer hours. You'll buy the house, but then you'll be in debt. Or maybe you won't want more, but once you do get what you want, you'll find yourself wondering, "now what?"

The good news is that you don't have to be unhappy with the struggle. If you can't be happy right here, right now, with what you have, then you'll never be happy even when you get more. That doesn't mean you can't get the house or promotion or whatever it is you want. It just means that you must accept where you are now and be okay with where you are now because once you get what you want, you're not going to be content with where you are at any point. You have to practice being okay with here and now. As one of my students would say, "Everyone else's burrito is always fuller." See your own burrito as being enough.

Activity

Pick a day to pay attention to what's demanding your attention. Every time something interrupts what you intend to do, write it down. At the end of the day, go through that list and find out which ones you can control by making changes. If there are some that you can't (I know you wish you could duct tape your toddler to their bed sometimes, but that's frowned upon) put that on your earlier list of things you can't control.

Chapter Fourteen: The Big Red F

When you were a child, did you ever receive a failing grade? If so, I bet it was a pretty devastating blow. If not, I'm sure you knew someone who had or had seen it happen to someone else. That sinking, horrible, life-ending feeling when the teacher hands you that paper with the Big Red F at the top, letting you know that you have done a terrible job. No doubt, your teacher would tell you how disappointed they were in you. And you had to quickly find a way to make an F look like an A before your parents saw it because you'd be in for it big time if they found out you failed.

We are taught from a young age that failure is bad. As a music and vocals teacher, I get kids and teens every day who walk into my room deathly scared to make a mistake. I see some wonderful creative talent held back by this fear of doing something wrong. This is heartbreaking to me. To watch children go through the school system riddled with anxiety, scared of that Big Red F because if they received it, the consequences were high.

In our society, failing is a bad word. We're not allowed to do it. If we fail in what we do, then we are a failure, and if we are a failure, then we are worthless, and we've already gone down this spiral many times before, haven't we?

It makes me laugh, in a sort of sad and desperate way, because we need to fail.

Failing keeps things interesting. If we succeeded at everything we did first try, what would be the fun in that? Sure, if you sat down at the piano and knocked out a Rachmaninoff Concerto with no practice, that might be a thrill at first. But after a while, it would make you yawn. Nothing would be worth it because there would be no surprise in it. You would know the moment you got into the cockpit of an airplane that you'd land it perfectly. You'd know the moment the cake went into the oven that it'd be delicious, and while that seems great on the surface, it would soon drive you insane because any amount of mystery would be taken out of life. We, as humans love a challenge; we thrive on it. Our big ol' mushy brains love learning, and as we've seen before, failing means learning.

Sometimes, when I come across obstacles in my path that can be frustrating. Sometimes I do have to go backward, circle around, and do something different than I had planned in the first place. That's okay. How boring would life be if it were just one straight, clear path with no obstacles, nothing changing, always just putting one foot in front of the other? I'd be bored out of my mind. And not the good kind of bored. We need obstacles in our path. We need a challenge because that's how we learn. It's how we keep from stagnating and becoming a blob of nothingness.

The roads we take in life are full of obstacles and failures. We see these things as something that gets in the way of living life, but they are a part of living life. As C.S. Lewis once wrote, "The great thing, if one can, is to stop regarding all the unpleasant things as interruptions of one's 'own,' or 'real' life. The truth is, of course, that what one calls the interruptions are precisely one's real life." [1]

Treating obstacles with curiosity rather than with frustration (though frustration is a valid response) can help us to discover different ways of looking at the world and can launch us into new ideas and approaches. Creativity loves that sort of thing. Our richness comes from the discovery of something new. Discovery comes from exploring the areas we have not previously explored.

Best of all, a path full of failure and obstacles reminds us that we are not in control. We cannot control every situation; if we could, things would get very boring again. Sometimes, we need this reminder to let go, lighten up, and stop going into mega-productivity mode when we don't need to be doing that. When we remind ourselves we're not in control of the little things, it makes it much easier to handle the big things when life throws a huge reminder our way.

When I was learning how to meditate, I learned that the idea of focusing on the breath was to create an anchor for attention. The idea was that if you lost focus on your breath a thousand times, you would bring your attention back a thousand and one times. It's not really a failure. It's part of the process. If you fall a thousand times, get up and dust yourself off a thousand and one times.

Chapter Fifteen: Working with Deadlines and Commitments

In the real world, there are things we have to do. We've got no choice. We may have a job with work and deadlines given to us. We may have kids that we have to take care of. We have bills to pay, groceries to buy, and cars to maintain. This is the society we live in. It seems like a lot—and it is.

But remember, needing to do work is natural. Animals have to hunt or scavenge for food, especially before winter sets in. They have to build nests and look after their young too.

The world doesn't sit still. It keeps moving, and we often have to move with it, whether we feel like it or not. But that's alright. We need some of that movement, that tension, and those required responsibilities to keep strong, healthy, and energetic. Remember, it's about balance. There are times of movement and times of rest. Welcome both into your life with equal gusto.

I'm no stranger to having to work overtime to make rent, getting into debt, and having to work long hours to make ends meet. This is an unfortunate symptom of our current economic system. This is your permission to be in the trenches and to not worry about making your bed or if you're making enough art to be considered an artist.

How to Work When You Have To

The following are a few tips on how to get something done even if you have to. This works best with bigger projects, but you can take some of this advice for smaller tasks as well.

1. Try the list on p 139 and see if you can pair your required tasks down to the vital minimum.

2. Ask yourself how you can make it easy. If you can get away with making a few items on your to-do list easier, then do it. Ask yourself if you have to do your tasks a specific way. If not, how can you make it easier on yourself?

3. Delegate if possible. This one can be especially hard, but if you feel you can't delegate something, ask yourself why. Sometimes you can't, but sometimes you may find that there's a mental or emotional block preventing you from handing the task off to someone else.

4. Do you really have to do the work? Sometimes we think we have to do something, but we really don't need to. We just feel like we do. Ask yourself if you truly need to do it. If you don't, let it go.

5. Put the deadline for the work on your calendar. Find out the minimum amount of work you can do each day to complete the task on time. Put some time in your calendar to do it. If you can, find the time of day you're most energetic and schedule it then. Take advantage of higher energy days so you can do more in case other days aren't ideal for working.

6. Just do the thing. Sometimes, the idea of doing something is harder than just doing it. I can't tell you how many times I've dreaded doing something for days, weeks, maybe months, and it turned out it was just some tiny little thing I could do in a day. Just do the thing. Then reward yourself with some rest.

Part Four: Sustainable Creativity

Chapter Sixteen: Turning Outward

I always thought of myself as a fairly empathetic person. Certainly, I did (and do) care for others, but I realized that when I felt upset, bored, uncreative, anxious, or depressed, every thought was about myself.

As I got out of bed in the morning, I thought about how tired I was and how hard it was for me to get out of bed. When I put on clothes, I thought of what others would think of me when I went out of the house. As I sat down to create, I thought about how I sounded and if others would like what I created. As I taught voice lessons in the evenings, I wondered if the children understood me and if they cared about what I was saying. As I cooked dinner for my kids, I wondered if they were even going to eat what I worked so hard to make.

Everything, even the depths of my depression and anxiety, was centered toward myself. I couldn't believe how self-centered I actually was! (and still am, it's a life-long journey I'm working on). I don't mean self-centered in a bad way like we usually portray it. I mean it literally. My thoughts were centered on myself, even when I was trying to help others.

It's a perfectly natural response to think inwardly when things aren't going smoothly. It's a form of self-preservation. The thought of "am I in danger?" can take many different forms in this modern world. We don't have to worry about being chased by tigers, but our brain can't really tell the difference between that and whether or not others are thinking not very nice things about us.

Yet, we are a social species, evolved to depend on each other for our very lives. Renowned anthropologist Sarah Blaffer Hrdy argues in her book *Mothers and Others: The Evolutionary Origins of Mutual Understandings* that humans have evolved to the point where we cannot survive as a species without social connection[1]. We rely both on getting and receiving help from others.

But our society celebrates individualism and isolation—our nuclear families in separate houses outlined by fences and borders surrounding neighborhoods, cities, and nations. Now, more than ever, in a post-COVID world, we have delved even deeper into individualism and isolation, pulling us deeper into ourselves.

It's easy to get pulled into that self-centered thinking, even if you don't mean to. But turning outward can help mental health and creativity. Studies have shown that empathy, selflessness, and acts of service can help heal the mind and ease anxiety and stress. A team of scientists at Yale School of Medicine published a study that showed that people who performed small acts of kindness mitigated the effects of stress and felt overall more positive.[2] By turning your attention to the care of others, you provide space in your mind for creativity.

The next time you find yourself trying to create and blocked with fear that the world will reject you, try turning your mental focus outward. Who in this world can you help with your creation? Who could benefit from a song, a poem, a drawing, a note no matter what? Create for them. This isn't for you. This is to put something good into the world that wasn't there before. And when you do create for someone else, notice how it feels as if the clouds clear, the muscles relax, and you can breathe just a little bit easier.

Chapter Seventeen: Productivity for a Better Cause

And here we come to the whole idea behind this book. There will no doubt be many who read the title, perhaps even the whole book, and say, "well, we can't just sit around and do nothing and waste away," or "productivity worked for me," or perhaps they'd like to tell me the parable of the ants and the grasshopper, the one where the grasshopper starves to death because he was too lazy to prepare for winter, unlike the hard-working ants.

The problem isn't that we're doing things. The problem is that we're doing things for the sake of doing things. Staying busy for the sake of staying busy, and if we're not staying busy, we feel guilty for not staying busy. We work hard just to stay relevant in a world where "getting ahead" and being better than average are rewarded.

Productivity for the sake of productivity is not productivity at all. It's the dog chasing its tail. But without the fun. And eventually, we're going to run ourselves into the ground and wonder why we feel overwhelmed and broken.

What should we be productive for, then? Again, I bring back the idea of turning away from the self and looking to others. What if, instead of trying to drive this busy-for-the-sake-of-busy machine into the ground, we turned our energies to something for the greater good? What could that be?

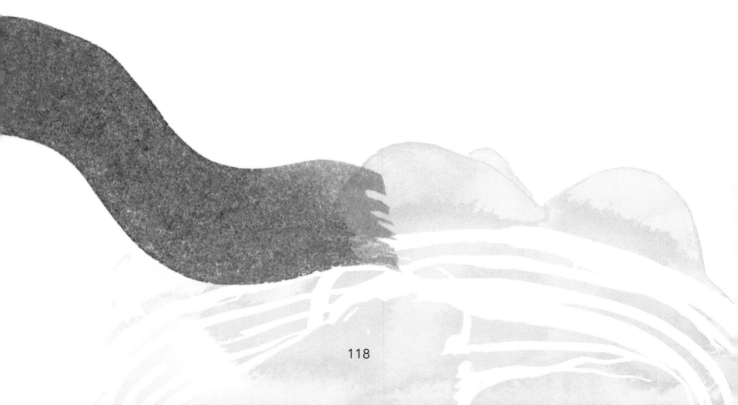

Well, that's where your compass comes into play. What matters to you? Does saving the planet for future generations to enjoy sound like a good cause? How about ending human trafficking and modern slavery? Getting orphaned children adopted? Opening doors for refugees? Free healthcare for all? Fresh fruit and vegetables available to everyone? There are so many things out there that would benefit humanity and the world in general. Suppose you put your energies when you have found the rhythms of your energetic cycles into these causes. In that case, productivity ceases to be the means to an end itself and becomes something actually productive. And think. If the whole world put its productivity and goal energies into this kind of work, how much better would our world be?

By creating, not to be productive for productivity's sake or to become better than average, but to help the world get just a little bit better, our work becomes more sustainable. We have a cause greater than ourselves, and we produce to thrive.

So sit and think for a moment. Journal, daydream, meditate, take a walk through your city or town, look through a newspaper, and see what gets our compass needle pointing north. What would you like to be productive for? I think, in the end, those are the real smart goals.

Conclusion

There's nothing wrong with wanting to cross some items off of your bucket list. Saving up for a trip, running a marathon, writing a book. All of these can be some great ways to experience life. If you are overwhelmed and constantly tired, I recommend you take some time and rest. Put these wish list items down for a while and focus on smaller things like going for walks, spending more time with family, or even just taking a few minutes each day to do something you want to do.

After resting and clearing your mind, you may find that you have more energy to tackle some of the bigger items. I say go for it! Give yourself permission.

However, the way we traditionally tackle goals tends to bring us back to a place of feeling overwhelmed and out of control. These goals are often based on things in life we can't control, like weather, an unexpected illness, or the behavior of others. Goals that require life to run smoothly often set us up for failure, disappointment, and anxiety.

1. Remember your compass. If you haven't done the compass exercise on p 91 already, I recommend you do that first. Ask yourself if this goal fits in with the direction you want to go. If not, I suggest you find a goal more suited to your values.

2. Get curious about your goal. Ask yourself why you want to do it. Then, when you have an answer, ask yourself why again. Keep asking why until you get down to that nugget of truth. You'll know it when you feel it.

3. Approach the goal as an experiment. If you tie this goal into your identity, anything that goes wrong will make you feel like a failure. Instead, look at your goal through the eyes of a scientist. Make observations rather than getting tied up in the story. What happens when you go for that goal? What happens if it doesn't work? No matter what, it was all part of the experiment.

4. Ask yourself: How can I make this easy? What areas of working on your goal can be made easier? Look for ways that will make you do the work rather than having a rigid set of plans.

5. Go with the flow. Some days we feel it; some days, we don't. That's okay. We're not machines. Set up a minimum of the tiniest of tasks to work toward this goal every day. If you do that minimum, then you are moving closer to the goal. If you have some energy, do a bit more. Remember, rest is a necessity and often helps us with goals. Be intentional with your rest.

Take a moment to appreciate where you've been. Once you finish the goal, savor the fact that you completed it. Congratulate yourself and make some space before you move on to another goal. Rest, and then return rejuvenated.

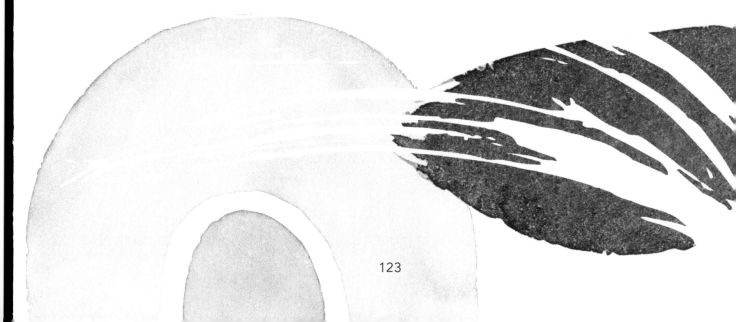

Stuff You Don't Have To Do

a. You don't have to take a cold shower to get energy
b. You don't have to eat foods you hate just because you think you have to
c. You don't have to have your place spotless. A little mess can be healthy
d. You don't have to do any kind of exercise you hate just because you think you're supposed to.
e. You don't have to be liked by everyone.
f. You don't have to like everyone.
g. You don't have to be on social media
h. You don't have to read books you don't like.
i. You don't have to have everything in order.
j. You don't have to know everything about a subject before you start
k. You don't have to make your bed
l. You don't have to fold your clothes as soon as the dryer finishes
m. You don't have to be happy all of the time
n. You don't have to be energetic all of the time

o. You don't have to buy that thing
p. You don't have to watch that show your friends want you to watch
q. You don't have to meal prep
r. You don't have to travel the world
s. You don't have to climb Mount Everest
t. You don't have to have an opinion on everything
u. You don't have to save the thing you love doing until you finish all the things you don't love doing.
v. You don't have to have ideas that make sense.
w. You don't have to be happy all of the time.
x. You don't have to have a "brand."
y. You don't have to.

Interview

A few months before publishing this book, I had the honor of taking a class taught by Kate Marolt at a wonderful event called Camp Nerd Fitness. Her class was all about creativity and working through the fear and doubt that are often intertwined with creating something. I was amazed at how closely her philosophy was to my own, I just had to pick her brain. She wonderfully took some time out to sit and have a chat with me. Here's what she had to say:

DEVYN: Can you explain how you approach creativity and your own creative works?

KATE: To me, we're always creating. We're literally always in a state of creation; our bodies are constantly creating. Creativity is the act of bringing something to life, whatever that is. When I think of that in terms of like a painting or a writing project, I see creative works as things that kind of have their own consciousness, their own desire to be in the world. I like to approach things from that perspective because the pressure isn't just on me.

Creativity is a living, breathing process. And so, as I work and create, I'll think about something and start to sort of outline it in my head or maybe on paper, and then I'll just jump right in the middle to where my brain wants to go and see what happens. I know there's a lot of privilege in saying this, but as much as possible, I try not to have intense deadlines that I create for myself for no reason. There's a lot of arbitrary deadlines, and then there are very real deadlines. We are all inherently creative. Creativity is an expression of being alive. So when I do create, it's like creating life in this way. I'm expressing the fact that I'm alive, and I have ideas and thoughts and things to get out.

DEVYN: So what do you do when you don't feel like it?

KATE: That has required a lot of practice and understanding. Sometimes it's like, "Oh, am I just not in the mood because I'm resisting something that's uncomfortable? I don't know what's going to happen in this creative session."

Do I need to eat something? Do I need to move my body for a little while, get some energy out? Is it because there's something physical that I need? Food? Water? To be in the sunshine? Move something for a little while? But I also think there's a lot of deeper inside stuff that I have to look at, like why don't I feel like it? Particularly, if I do actually have physical energy and it's like, okay, what am I resisting? Like, what am I worried about? What am I trying to protect myself from by not stepping into my creative work and doing something?

I'm somebody who requires a lot of validation, so if I'm in an uncomfortable place in what I'm creating and I'm not sure how it's going to be received, a lot of times, that's when I don't feel like it. So if I'm in my head, I have to look at where I can actually ground into myself and reconnect to the vision that I had and the excitement I have for my work. Or full permission to just sit down and create and then throw it all out that day. Sometimes you have to sit down and do it when you don't feel like it and see what happens. And sometimes I'll wait all day and be like, "I can't go to bed unless I do something," because it will just be racing around in my brain.

DEVYN: I like the idea that sometimes it's something so physically simple that we forget we need to like eat and we need to sleep, and we will often put those things aside first as if they're not as important as whatever needs to be done when they're really the thing that needs to be done the most.

Say you've eliminated the immediate physical needs or the feeling that you're scared of a particular thing. How do you determine, "Okay, it is time for me to step back and not be hard on myself today or not push myself today." As opposed to a day where you're like, "Okay, I'm making excuses. I need to just sit my butt down and do something."

KATE: It's not going to be a cut-and-dry answer, but a lot of times, there are certain things I look at like if I don't feel safe for some reason. Whatever that reason is, I will do work with my nervous system and take some time to settle, regulate and tune in to what's going on in my body because creation is such an embodied act. We think it's all in our heads, but for me, it's a whole self-experience that includes my body. Often avoidance is like some sort of protection mechanism happening in my body. So I will take some time to be with that and create a sense of safety within myself first.

The other thing that I like to look at is if I don't feel safe, whatever I create right now isn't going to come from a place that works for me. That's when I decide to take a step back. Sometimes, and I say these things very lightly because they could be taken in ways that I wouldn't actually align with, but how am I going to feel about myself at the end of the day if I don't create? But I put that in a broader context of if I'm exhausted, and I really need a nap instead of going to create something, not honoring myself is not the same thing as what's actually self-honoring is to create today. I think it's a nuanced question, a complex thing that needs to be different for everybody.

A quick example is, in the past, there have been things that happened in the world I would have had a reaction like "I have to write something, I have to say something, I have to prove I'm a good person, I have to be outraged, do all these things" Right? And then what I was saying over the weekend [is] I have things I want to express and share that feel really honoring for me that's not coming from a pressured need to prove anything. I have something that I want to express, and I don't need it to be expressed in any particular way, but it's a felt sense more so than it is anything else.

DEVYN: I like what you were saying about feeling safe and everything being embodied, so I guess there's part of creativity in your eyes that's just learning how to be more in tune with your body and what you're feeling and just observing it more than judging it.

KATE: Yeah. If you can have regard for yourself instead of disregarding your needs and your fears and your feelings - if I had to give you a key, that would be it. I know it's a big thing to ask, but that is the work that creates the space to try new things, to be scared and do it anyway, and you can hold yourself in it.

DEVYN: What do you do when you're too scared to create?

KATE: My go-to is I will move energy out of my body, whether that's going for a run or just hitting stuff [laughs]. A big thing that I do because my fear response is often to freeze, so I counteract that sometimes with very gentle movement so I don't always go for a run. When I feel that energy building up in my system, it's usually a sign to not keep trying to create what I'm creating but to go move that energy, go do something. The worst thing I can do is go and sit on the couch and distract myself.

All that is physiological, right? Whether it's fight, flight, or freeze, our systems get keyed up to do something, so it's giving that energy an outlet to run itself through and reset your system. Sometimes it can be like, "I'm afraid, let me try and figure out why I'm afraid, let me do all this mental exercise." And while that's happening, your body is just coursing with adrenaline, or it's stuck and can't move. Let me get that out of my system first and then see where I end up.

DEVYN: Do you have anything else to add about courage, energy, and creativity?

KATE: My favorite topics. I really see courage as the capacity to share and express and speak what's in your heart. And that takes practice. It's also not something that happens in spite of fear; it's not being fearless. Courage and fear can walk hand in hand together. When you contend [with] your fear, that's when courage can come through and give you that energy and space to try something out, see where it goes. I also feel the more comfortable you can be with uncertainty and doubt and not knowing what's going to happen, I wouldn't say the easier it is to create, but the more capacity there is to create. If you're constantly seeking certainty, that takes out the mystery of creation.

To find out more about creativity and self-honoring,
you can find Kate at katemarolt.com
And on Instagram: @kate_marolt

Book Recommendations

- *Start Where You Are* by Pema Chodron

- *Steal Like an Artist* by Austin Kleon

- *Daring Greatly* by Brene Brown

- *The Creative Habit* by Twyla Tharp

- *Your Illustrated Guide to Becoming One With the Universe* by Yumi Sakugawa

- *The Artist's Way* by Julia Cameron

- *The Wander Society* by Keri Smith

- *How to Do Nothing* by Jenny Odell

Notes

Chapter One:

1. Chamorro-Premuzic, Tomas, Ph.D. "The Upsides of Being Average." *Psychology Today*, 2 June 2017, https://www.psychologytoday.com/us/blog/mr-personality/201706/the-upsides-being-average.
2. Watts, Alan. *The Wisdom of Insecurity: A Message for an Age of Anxiety*. Vintage Books: A division of Random House, Inc. New York, February 2011.

Chapter Two:

1. Belk, Russell W. "Possessions and the Extended Self." Journal of Consumer Research, vol. 15, no. 2, 1988, pp. 139–68, http://www.jstor.org/stable/2489522. Accessed 13 April 2022.
2. Milyavskaya, M., Saffran, M., Hope, N. *et al*. Fear of missing out: prevalence, dynamics, and consequences of experiencing FOMO. *Motiv Emot* 42, 725–737 (2018). https://doi.org/10.1007/s11031-018-9683-5

Chapter Four:

1. Frankl, Victor, E. Man's Search for Meaning. 1959. Translated by Ilse

Lasch. Better Yourself Books, 2006.

2. TEDxTalks. "The Art of Creativity | Taika Waititi | Tedxdoha." YouTube, YouTube, 4 Nov. 2010, https://www.youtube.com/watch?v=pL71KhNmnls.

3. Chodron, Pema. Start Where You Are: A Guide to Compassionate Living. Shambhala Publications, Inc, 1994.

4. TEDxTalks. "The Power of Vulnerability | Brené Brown | TEDxHouston." YouTube, YouTube, 6 Oct. 2010, https://www.youtube.com/watch?v=X4Qm9cGRub0.

Chapter Seven:

1. He, Q., Turel, O. & Bechara, A. Brain anatomy alterations associated with Social Networking Site (SNS) addiction. Sci Rep 7, 45064 (2017). https://doi.org/10.1038/srep45064.

2. Reed, Phil. "Anxiety and Social Media Use." Psychology Today, 3 Feb. 2020, https://www.psychologytoday.com/us/blog/digital-world-real-world/202002/anxiety-and-social-media-use.

Chapter Eight:

1. Almendrala, Anna. "Lin-Manuel Miranda's Greatest Idea Came to Him on Vacation." HuffPost, HuffPost, 23 June 2016, https://www.huffpost.com/entry/lin-manuel-miranda-says-its-no-accident-hamilton-inspiration-struck-on-vacation_n_576c136ee4b0b489bb-0ca7c2.

Chapter Eleven:
1. Frankl, Victor, E. Man's Search for Meaning. 1959. Translated by Ilse Lasch. Better Yourself Books, 2006.
2. O'Brien, Conan. *"Conan O'Brien Needs a Friend: President Brack Obama."* Podcast, May 30, 2021.
3. https://brenebrown.com/resources/dare-to-lead-list-of-values/

Chapter Fourteen:
1. Lewis, C.S. *The Collected Works of C.S. Lewis.* World Publishing, 1996.

Chapter Sixteen:
1. Hrdy, Sarah Blaffer. *Mothers and Others: The Evolutionary Origins of Mutual Understanding.* 1946. The Belknap Press of Harvard University Press, 2009.
2. Raposa, Elizabeth B., et al. "Prosocial Behavior Mitigates the Negative Effects of Stress in Everyday Life." Clinical Psychological Science, vol. 4, no. 4, July 2016, pp. 691–698, doi:10.1177/2167702615611073.

Interview
1. Kate Marolt is a coach, mentor, and facilitator who creates spaces for your whole self to come alive and thrive. Since 2011 she has been supporting smart, creative humans to tune into the wisdom of their bodies, build self-love and self-trust, and bring their full

range of gifts and expression online so they can create lives based in joy and deep fulfillment.

2. Camp Nerd Fitness is a recurring event put on by the team at nerd-fitness.com. You can find out more at camp.nerdfitness.com/

3. nterview was edited for print with permission

Acknowledgments

I'd like to thank all the people involved in helping and supporting me in writing this book. Thank you to Lindsey Smith, Alex Franzen, Woz Flint, Tracie Kendziora, and all of the team at Get it Done, who put in so much work and patience as I waffled more times than I should have over what the heck I wanted to say to the world. A special thanks to Tracie, who reminded me this is an average book for average creators, so maybe I shouldn't stress over perfectionism. Thank you to my Rebel Sisters, who encouraged and cheered me on. Thank you to my students and colleagues who gave me inspiration and support. And thank you to my husband, Owen, who helped me to clarify my message and never once doubted me.

Author Bio

Devyn Fraser Price is the vocal director at the School of Rock in Cypress, Texas. This is her first book, though probably not her last. Devyn has a Bachelor of Arts in Creative Writing and History from the University of Houston and an Associate of Arts in Music from Lone Star College. She currently lives in Houston, Texas, with her husband, two children, and two dogs.

CPSIA information can be obtained
at www.ICGtesting.com
Printed in the USA
BVHW061547200123
656705BV00006BA/51

9 781956 989182